Every day in the morning

(slow)

Every day in the morning

(slow)

Adam Seelig

NCOUVER   NEW STAR BOOKS   2010

New Star Books Ltd.
107 — 3477 Commercial Street, Vancouver, BC V5N 4E8   CANADA
1574 Gulf Road, No. 1517, Point Roberts, WA 98281   USA
www.NewStarBooks.com   info@NewStarBooks.com

Publication of this work is made possible by the support of the Government of Canada throug
the Canada Council and the Department of Canadian Heritage Book Publishing Industry De
opment Fund, and the Province of British Columbia through the British Columbia Arts Counci
and the Book Publishing Tax Credit.

Cover by Clint Hutzulak / Mutasis.com
Printed on 100% post-consumer recycled paper
Printed and bound in Canada by Gauvin Press
First printing, October 2010

LIBRARY AND ARCHIVES CANADA CATALOGUING IN PUBLICATION

Seelig, Adam, 1975–
   Every day in the morning (slow) / Adam Seelig.

Poems.
ISBN 978-1-55420-051-1
   I. Title.

PS8637.E444E84 2010   C811'.6   C2010-901792–7

When he appears on the ~~stage~~ page, besides what he actually is doing he will at all

essential points discover, specify, imply what he is not doing; that is to say he will act in

such a way that the alternative emerges as clearly as possible, that his acting allows the

other possibilities to be inferred and only represents one out of the possible variants. In this

way every ~~sentence~~ letter and every ~~gesture~~ word signifies a decision.

Bertolt Brecht *modified*

                                                                sink under
                    the mirror
                    where   still
                              in
                              the
     dark   he

ubs his sometimes
          sore   hands before washing them
                    and   wetting
     his   cheeks
                    and
     chin   and   stubble
                    and   with
     his   hands
                    a   little
          sore
out   only
                    a   little
                                        he
outs   on
          some   shaving   cream picks
                                        up
     his   razor blade
                    and
                    starts   shaving
                              in   the

yellow light he's flicked on a
          slightly
yellow light   that
               flickers   at   first above
                              the   mirror
                              that
          reflects   him
ell   what   else

This
  is what
    happens in the morning of course many things
    happen   to   many   people
        in the morning   but
this
  is what
    happens

when Sam wakes up it's
          still dark
            in
the   window
         and
        still
           in
the   room since Layla has left

  for
work like the
    neighbours upstairs all gone to
work   to
      be   together
         with   others leaving

Sam to wake alone and
    walk   past the window by
        the piano
             over
to   the   bathroom its cool
               floor
            cools his feet
        covering
      the
same   steps fro
      bed

can

a   mirror

do   but

reflect   and

what   else

can   you

do   in

the   mirror   but   face

your

face

and

reflect   on

how   you

used to believe you could write

music to   make a living simply

make a living   from

writing

your   own God

how   naive

you   were

to believe   that back

then but

then   you passed

the   ideal age

to   become

a   famous

composer

the   idea   of

fame   never

came

to   pass

and   now

as   more   time goes on

you

can't seem to sell your music
   no   matter what
       it   doesn't
   seem to sell
      or   bring
                            in
any   money   nothing

this year not
    one   piece   sold
             or
      picked   up
         or   commissioned while
he   does fine all
the   same because whatever
                          Father wants
                          Father gets
              with all
the   money
he
has

for what
for   sitting
for   sitting on his rump   all day
                  as   if
      his
  fat   ass
       shits   bills
           all day
     long   a
        trumpet call   of bills from
      his   ass
          as   if   from out
          of
     his

fat   ass   pops

            one

            long trumpet

that   toots

                      bills

            all day

         long

for   just

    sitting   since

       he   just

    sits   on his   ass

         all day   like

              me   i   guess

              a   little

                      like

           me

           so

what   if   i

        also

   sit

when i work

   i   really

   work

   i   don't just

   sit

and   get fat

  if   anything

  i'm   getting   even thinner

    really

  i work   when

  i

  sit   at the   piano

    well ok

  i   write

           when

                i
        sit   at the   piano
                            ok   sometimes
        i   write
                                                when

        i
        sit
        and   sometimes
        i   just
        sit
        and   think
                                at the   piano
when   my
        hands   are
                        too   sore
                        to
                play
        and   compose
                                                                        so
        i   just   hold
                                them
        and   rub
                                them
        and   don't   write
                                anything
                        down or
                                                                        sometimes
        i   write
                        down just

one note that's it
one   stroke
        on   the page
                that's it stroke   smoothly
                                he   said

make   your skin

smooth as

a   baby

he   said

and

you're   still

my

baby

he   said

my

only

he   said

ever

since

your   mother

you

know

he   said   but

stopped   and

then   said

stroke   as

smoothly

as   you   can

that's it   the   smoother   your

strokes

the   smoother

the

shave

that's it

only

one note

one note

one note   but

then

maybe

one note   is

all it
    takes why not
    like   Cage
              one
                note
                  to
                  be
    like   John
                Cage
          or Riley repetitive
    like   Terry
                Riley   what
a   bore
        why not
        bore   me
                to   death
    like   Cage
          or Riley
        why   is
                Terry
                Riley   so
                  repetitive
a   bore
    like   Reich
    take
a   bore
    like   Steve
                Reich   is Philip Glass
                            as
              repetitive   you wonder
                            as   you
                  shave   in
                        the   mirror

                                    is

            one
                note
all it
      takes
                for   me
                  to
                  be   the   next
                                                    Glass
            or Reich
            or Riley
            or Cage   sure
        if   what   you want
                                              is
                  to
                  be
  a   bore
  a   famous
            bore   mind
                                                      you
                      but
  a   bore
  all   the   same
        why are
                                          they
  all   the   same
                                                    and
        why   is
            one
            more   repetitive than   the   next
                                          is
    it
            to
            bore   me
            to   death

m
a
y
b
e

it   is
 like
it   or
            not
                   but
it

sells because
      a   style
sells   and if
                 it
sells   it has power
          and   power
sells   art
   because   art
                has no
                power but
              the power   to
sell   style   since
                     art   let's face
          it   is
     a   sham
          and
          an   artist
                  is   nothing
                     but
     a   ham   with ease for
        style   yes
                                         ease

              power

and

a   cheap

and   cheesy

style   to

sell

because   the   cheesier

the

style   the more

it

sells   pathetic

i have

no

style   to

sell   and   no

power   to

sell   it

all   i have   is   my   pathetic

music

at least you make something

Layla says

playing   with

my   hair and she's got

a   point

at least you make

your

music   what does

he

make   what   exactly

does

he   do

anything   other

than

play   the

market   and

has   he   ever

created   anything

in   his   life

like

you   do   or

played   the

piano   like

you

she

says

but i haven't made

any   money

this   year

i   **say**

what   about

the

new   piece you've been working

on

she

says

it's   just

on   spec

i   **say**

and stuck

i   **say**

what

she

says

i'm   stuck

i   **say**

come

on   Sam

i'm   sure

you're   just

making   slow

progress
she says
        i wrote
            one
            note yesterday
        i
    say
                    you
    see   that's
progress
    she says
                            even
        if   it's   just
            one
            note   you're   still making music
    she's   got   a   point
        i
guess
                                            seriously
                        what   exactly does
    he   make
    she says

a lot
    of money   that's
        what
            i say
                yes
                    she
            says
        that's
all   he

                makes so   why not
let   him   help
                us   out
                she
                says
                            no
                    way
            i say
                    why not
                she
                says
                                        too
        many   strings attached
                i say
        come
        on   Sam baby
                    we   could   really
            use
            it
                            not
        from   him   no
                                not
            with
all   his   strings attached
                                    but   hey
            that's
business   that's
            what   being
                a
business   man
                is   for
                to
push   others around
            with   money
                    and

                to be   around
        a   lot
                        of   money
        with
        a   lot
                        of   other
business   men
but   not
        a   lot
                        of
                women
    since   women   are
                               the
                        other   money
                        of
                men
    in
business

turning women
            into plastic
                    tits with
                elastic   thighs
                    skin   so
                        tight   you can see through
                                and
                    it   all gets worse
        when   the
        women   getting   pushed around
                                                                    start
                                                                pushing
                                other
        women   around
                                    not
            to   mention

babies we can't afford
          and
    she   knows
    we can't afford
    them   even though
    she   would love some
          of
    her   own
       and
       aren't
    they   delicious
    she   says
       aren't
    they   to
die   for
                        but
  i   can't afford
            to   let
    her and   if
  i
did   would
    she   leave
                                me
                  here
                  with
       it
  i   mean
    she can't afford
    the   time
       to   be
                  with
  a
baby   or   would
    she   leave

16

                              with
                  it
      i   can't   let
          her   leave
                      or

make
me   a
        father   or
                  worse first
          a   husband i'm not
          the   fathering
                  or   husbanding type
                          and

what if she died having
            the   baby

it never happens
    she   tells
      me   but
    it   did
                            but
    she   was one
              in
          a   million cases
it's   so   rare
    she   tells
    me   so   should
i   feel
              better   Mother being
                      one
              in
          a   million   doesn't make
    me   feel

better   and   doesn't

she

get enough babies
    in
        the   bloody maternity ward can't she
get   her
        baby   fix
                                    there
                    at   work   like all
        the   other   OBs
                                and

aren't
    i   baby enough for her what
            do
    i   need
                        to   cry
                for her   to   care
            more   don't
    i   need
                her
        enough   and
            she
        can   barely afford
                            me
        a   resident
        can   barely   make
        enough   to   support
            us   both
                                and

    i

wish

she'd stop about his money almost begging for
            his money
            while
        you

shave the way
        he
showed me   to
                face
        the   mirror hold
        his   hand
                        and watch
how   he   feels
        his   face   holds
        the   razor
                        and   sees
        me   in
        the   mirror
now   razor
                in   hand   smile
                                so   much like
        his   smiling
                        and
                    holding   my
                    hand
            to
        his   face   before
        he   pushed
        me
            away
when   for
        a   moment
                    i   touched
        his

                                                                              b
                                                                              l
                                                                              a
                                                                              d
                                                                              e

                    it   was   just   for
          a   moment
                                                   but
    the   moment
                    i   touch
                    it   my
                              hand

bleeds   and i know
              it   was stupid
    and i   think
              i   cried when
                                    he said
                                              that
                        was stupid
    and   then
                                              just
                              be   sure not
                                              to
bleed   to   death
                                                               Jesus
                                              just don't
bleed   to   death
                                   is   that   supposed
                                              to
                        be   one
                                                                       of
                              his
          stupid   jokes
                              is

20

                              her   death
                                           just
                a   joke
                                    to
              him
              i   mean
                                                  Jesus
              i   know
              it   was stupid   of   me
              and   now

i'm feeling sentimental look
i   have
    feelings
              fine
i   have
    feelings   and
i'm   fine   with
          sentiment   and
              fine with
    feeling   confused
                          now
                and   then   but
                                    to
    feel   sentimental
          as
i   do   to
    feel   sentimental
          as
i   do
    at   the
          moment
is   to
    be   weak
              mentally   weak

and

mental   weakness

is   a   virus

of

the

mind   that   spreads

to

the   body

and

hands

until   you're

too

weak

to   bear   more

any

feelings   or

children

and   to

have   the   weakness

of

a   child's   body

of   your mother's

body

a

kind   of

weakness

for

feeling   weak

is   a

sentimental   disease

but

to

love is another
        matter to

love   to sing
      as Father   claims
                          she
loved   to sing
      is   different
                        even
                        if
            he   can't

remember any of the songs
                she sang why
      can't   he   learn
        a   simple melody that
        a   simple   idiot could
                        learn
                who
      can't   learn
        a   simple melody
        a   melody that
                              his
                  own   wife
            sang
        no   less
                  who
      can't
remember   that
        an   idiot
                                            that's
                  who
        an   idiot   without
        an   ear
        an   idiot   without
        a   memory
                                or
        a

man   without

    a

mother

because i can't recall then but

    then

    i   wasn't even born

      yet   for God's

          sake

    of   course

    i can't recall   so   what

    can

be   his   excuse

          what excuse

    can   he   have

          that

    he

    can't recall the

melody the words yes

    he   has

    a

memory   for

    the words   and

    for   numbers

    a   better

memory   for   numbers but

    a   person with

    no

memory   for

melody   is

    no   better

    than

    a   bird

    that

                    can't   twitter
        yes   no   better
            than
            a   bird brain
            a   person with
            a   brain
    for   numbers
            and
        words   but
                not
        for
melody   has   shit
        for   brains
            and   all
    the   numbers   upon
                numbers
            and
        words   upon
        words   if
                not
        for
melody   would
                                        all

                    be
        for

nothing like Clapping Music Steve
                    Reich's
        Clapping Music
nothing   to
                        it
                        it's
    like   a   machine
                    that's
        all

clap
clap
clap
clap

                so
            what   anyone
                      can

   clap   what   makes
            that so   brilliant
            that   there's
nothing   to
            it
            that   anyone
                      can
            do
            it
            is
            that
            what   makes
         Steve
         Reich's
Clapping Music   brilliant   Father
                      can
    clap   so
               is   Father
a   musical   genius
                                  when
all   he
                      can
            do
            is   make
     money
no   what
            is   brilliant
            is

that
Steve
Reich's
music   makes
money   too
while   you
and   your
music   make
nothing   Steve
Reich   is
a   money   making
machine
that's   raking
it
in like   Father
clap
clap   and
money
simply

appears one day
he
appears
to
be   talking
to   himself
so   i   ask
him
what   he's
talking   about
it's
a   song
she   used
to   sing
he

says

        can

     you

 sing   it

to

 me

  i   ask

   him

    you   know

  i   can't

  sing

   he

says   it's   true

   he   can't

  sing a   tune

to   save

   his   life

  then would

   you   tell

   it

to

 me   please

  i   ask

  she'd   want

 me

to   know

   it

too   wouldn't

  she

  i

say

   it's just

  a   silly folk

   song   Sam.

  he

says

at   least

tell

me   the   words

i   must   have

said   i

wonder if the Broadcast Corp
would   have

a   recording

of

it   maybe

if

i   write

to

one   of their   all request shows

maybe

one   of their   know

it   all

DJ's   will

play

it

i   doubt

it   but

i

could   still   send

in

a   request

dear so
and
so
do
you know that song
that   my father can't

                    sing   but
                  my mother   did before
                        she   died   having
                  me   and if
      you
      do
      could
      you   please play
                                  it
            thanks
            that'd   be   great
      oh   and

it's my birthday on April first
i   know
                  what you're thinking
            April   Fool but
i'm   serious
it'd   mean
                        a
            lot   to   me
                  if   you'd   play
it   on   my
      birthday   .   and
                  if   you   don't
                  have
it   which
                  i   doubt
                        you   do

then please play Stravinsky's Rite of Spring
                        "Le Sacre du Printemps"

my partner and i

my partner   what

          is   this business

           what

          is   she

my   business

  partner   even love now

          is

    a   business any how

my partner and i   love   each other

          love   your

          show

          love   .the   Rite

          of   Spring

and

          love   to make

          love   to

        . each other   like wild

donkeys thrusting our pelvises

      or   is   it

        pelvi

donkey   style while we listen

      to   the music mount

      and   surge

      so wow

        how great

    it'd   be

    if

    you

    would

play the Sacrificial Dance movement

    "Danse   Sacrale"

      as   performed

stiffly and with utter lack
  of   feeling by one
  of   our
                                        country's mediocre
              hack   orchestras
      its   institutional
                                        mediocrity   second
                        only   to
                                        our

so called healthcare system that can't keep
                                    a   birthing woman from
                        bleeping
                        bleeding
                  to
      death   come
                                            on   now really
      do   i   have
                  to   beg you

please
        i said
                at
  least   tell me
                  the words
please
please
please
        and   he   did
        i   guess
                  he   had
              a
heart   for   once
                        so   right
                                    there

and   then
       he   told
     me
   all   the
         words
    he   knew
                           to
                       the   song
    he   says
                 she   used
                   to   sing

one little kid
one little kid Father bought
 me
one little kid   then
            a   cat
                          eats
        the
     kid
        that
        Father bought
 me
one little kid   then
            a   dog bites
        the   cat
      that   eats
        the
     kid
      that   .
        Father bought
 me
one little kid   then
            a   stick
                beats

     the   dog

  that   bites

     the   cat

  that   eats

     the

kid

  that

  Father bought

me

one little kid   then   fire burns

     the   stick

  that   beats

     the   dog

  that   bites

     the   cat

  that   eats

     the

kid

  that

  Father bought

me

one little kid   then   water puts

                                  out

     the   fire

  that   burns

     the   stick

  that   beats

     the   dog

  that   bites

     the   cat

  that   eats

     the

kid

  that

  Father bought

me

one little kid   then   an ox

                                                                          drinks

        the   water

        that   puts

                                                     out

        the   fire

        that   burns

        the   stick

        that   beats

        the   dog

        that   bites

        the   cat

        that   eats

        the

    kid

        that

        Father bought

me

one little kid   then   a   butcher

    kills   the   ox

        that   drinks

        the   water

        that   puts

                                                     out

        the   fire

        that   burns

        the   stick

        that   beats

        the   dog

        that   bites

        the   cat

        that   eats

        the

    kid

                that
                Father bought
me
one little kid   then   an   angel
    kills   the   butcher
                that
    kills   the   ox
                that   drinks
                the   water
                that   puts
                                                out
                the   fire
                that   burns
                the   stick
                that   beats
                the   dog
                that   bites
                the   cat
                that   eats
                the
        kid
                that
                Father bought
me
one little kid   then
                the   "Holy
One"
    kills   the   angel
                that
    kills   the   butcher
                that
    kills   the   ox
                that   drinks
                the   water
                that   puts

36

                                                                out
            the   fire
        that   burns
            the   stick
        that   beats
            the   dog
        that   bites
            the   cat
        that   eats
            the
    kid
        that
            Father bought
 me
one little kid
one little kid

figures it all starts
        with   Father
                        the
                        father
figure   starts   not just
                        any   chain but
        a   chain
            of   death for God's
                                            sake

                        and
                    when   does
                    he   die
                    where   does
                    Father
figure   in
                    the   chain
                    other   than
                    at

the
start Father
at
the
start
with   God

at
the end
the   son
forsaken

and
Mother   neglected while
God

and
Father   in
the end
are   left

untouched by a
fucked   composition
of   their own making
compose   for
me
she   says
write
one   for
me   Sam
she   says

come   on   Sam   baby
she   says
do
you   want
me
to   massage

your   hands
                                              God yes please
                    it'll   make
you   feel
                                        · good
              she   says
              then
          come   here   and
touch   me
touch   me
touch   me
                     my

artiste
    she says it's a
              game
    she   likes me to play
    the
artiste   which
    is   to   say
    the   seducer because
art   seduces   and
              to   seduce
    is   a   sort
                   of
art   yes
    she   likes me to play
    the   "seducer
artiste"   which
    is   to   say
    the   pervert
                              because
    the
artist
    is   a   pervert

                    of
            sorts   who
                      plays
        games   and   perverts nature
                    for
    the
art   of
        it   and
                          whose   nature
        it
is   to   treat
                                                        nature
        like a
            game   as
        if   nature
    is
    there   for
                me to   seduce   yet   nature clearly
                              seduces
    the
artist   so
    the
artist   has
                    to   pervert nature
                                                    in   return
                                    because
    the
artist   or   as
    she likes   to say
    the
artiste   which
    is   to say
    the   pervert
                                    can   only
            resort

                    to

              games

        like

  the   game

  she   seduces

              me to play

                    for

    her

                            seduce

              me

              my

artiste

    she   says

                            seduce

              me

    the   way

        i

      like

      it

    she   says

    then

take off your clothes

                    i

                  say

take off your   cross

                    i

                  say

                            turn on

          the   radio and

                    uncross

      your

legs

      i say just like that

just like that

i say

as

if   to read

it   off   a

        page or

as

if   she

          were

    that   page   herself

        a

        page

     of

legs   in

       a   book

     to

     spread   open

       and   enter

       a   book   writ large

       and

     spread   open   for my

       pen   my admittedly

         large

       pen

     to   write

       in

      pages

    of

legs   spread   open   for me

       and   for

      her   and   for

   us

   just

   us

as   she

says

nothing more than
        yes
        is all she needs to
         tell me   for
           me   to know
    that   all she needs
        is   me
      and
nothing more than   me   alone
    that's   all   one
      yes   for
        me   to know
    that   she   only
          needs
        me
      well   maybe
          for
        the   time
                being   admit
                    it
              maybe
    that's
not   all she needs   maybe
        there
  are   times
        she needs
        me   to   be
more   man
   than   the   man   i
        am
        now   i   mean
      maybe
    she needs

other

men   i

hate   to

think   it

makes   me   want

to   puke but

for   now

at   least

for

the   time

being

all she needs

is   me   to   know

that   she   wants

nothing more than

my head between her hips

lips on

her lips

between her hip bones

where

her hips   and

the   slit   of

the   lips

between her hips   form

a   triangle

for

my   round

head between her hips   a   circle

on   a   triangle

for

the   tip   of

my   tongue

to

slip

                between
   the   slit   of
   the   lips
        between her hips
                where
my   tongue   circles
                                         around
                        and   angles
           her lips
                             to
              slip   inside
           her
head   on
              hips   circle
              on   triangle
           lips on
           lips   and
           the   tongue   inside

saying
       la
       la
       la
       la
       without a word
saying
       la
       la
       la
   in   her
   lap
   in   a   tongue
              she   knows well
       a   language
                             we

all
know   within after
all   i'm
a   thin   man
in

her
la
la
lap   tongue   beneath
her   hair wetting
my

chin
it's grown again
grown a
row   of stubble
and   looks dirty
and   i   hate
to   scratch
her with
the
stubble   that's
grown   and   spread like
a

disease
come up
she says so i
do
knock
knock
i
say

we all have our childish moments don't
we

                              knock
                              knock
                              i
                 say
come   in
             she says
                       so i
come
                       in
                              and
              then
              she says
                       knock
            me up
                                      but this
                       i   imagine really
                       you   imagine   that
              she says
                       knock
            me up

crass
    as it sounds

                              and
as   you   fill
            her   and   fill
                              with   love
            yes   love
    is   the   only   word
                                                          for
                              it   really

you   wonder

                if

you're   putting

your

disease   in

        her   too

        sick

as it sounds

                since

    it's

a   sort

                of disease that makes your

    hands   sore

        and   weak

a   disease   inherited from   Mother

                because   Mother's

                                weakness

    is   in

                            your   nature

        and

            sick

as it sounds

    it

    is   this

disease   in

            your   nature

                                    that

            you   love

                    and   mother

                    and

                    want

        her to   nurture

                    and   that

you   imagine

you   put

              in

     her

as   you

   come   into

     her   and   wonder

                                        if

     you knock

   her

up   since

    she   would

                                     love

        to

     be

              a   mother

                                             wouldn't

    she   love   for

     you

        to   fulfill

     her   wish

        to

become   a   mother at last

     the   mother of

              a

needy child of her own because
     children   are
needy   a
needy
greedy   plague
              a   sleep robbing money hungry
                              plague   yet
        when
        they   play

                    how   can   you resist
          them

with
    their perfect skin you can see why parents would
                        want   such
        perfect skin   and   when
    they   want
                to   touch that smooth
                skin
                to
        be   skin
                to
                skin
with
    their   child
                to   touch
    their   kin
with
    their   skin   as
    it   were
                you can see why parents
                    can't   help   but love
    their   children
    if   love
                                        is
    the   only
                                word
                                for
    it   because
                you   are
                        a
            kind
            of   child
                                    at

heart and when you
   can't   resist what
           you
hear   when   as
            it   were
     the   inner child
            in
     your   mind's
 ear   plagues
     you
     you

write
  it down compose
  it   to calm yourself
   down   breathe relax
         your   hands
    compose   yourself   don't
              try
      to   be
       a   virtuoso
            when
       you
write
  it down   you   don't   care
      to   be
       a   virtuoso
    composer   anyhow
     all you   care
      to   do   is
   slow
   down   and
write   what
      you
   compose   with

  care

                                      not

                    to

show
        off like those pimply little prodigies even though you
                                                could
show
        off like those   little
showoffs   if   you wanted to with
                                                    a
                        little prod   you
                                    could   play anything
                those   little
showoff   prodigies   play   for sure
                                              you
                                    could   play anything
                                    you want
        like   Lang
                                                                        Lang
                                                                  that
                        little
showoff   playing the

piano with
        his eyes closed
    and   greasy skin
                                making
        it   look
                    easy   to   play Rachmaninoff without
                even   looking
        he   plays
        the   prodigy
                    of   schmaltz
        why   not   fill

                        my
            ears   with
      it   go
                                                      on
                                                Lang
                                                Lang
                                                      go
                                                      on
and   pour
                  Schmaltzmaninoff
      right   into
                  my
            ears
and   why   not
add   herring
                  to
      it   go
            ahead   fill our
            ears   with
            greasy   schmaltz   herring
                                    you

            pimply little prodigy
      like   that

kiss
ass
Kissin or
kids   the world over

murdering Beethoven's Für Elise
                  la
                  la
                  la
                  la

la
la
la
la
la
                poor
Beethoven   what
    have   they done to you
                        it   should
    be   for
          Therese   anyway
    Für
      Therese   not
    Für   Elise   poor
                poor
  Beethoven
        even   your handwriting
misunderstood   by

              little   prodigies   playing
                                    with
                              a
          skill
      people
    would   die   for
                            but
who   likes   prodigies
who   likes
  showoffs   even   a
              little   and
who
  show   me
who   likes   pimply

teenagers at least little kids

are   still   sincere despite

all   their

germs   as   opposed

to   spiteful

teenagers   still

too   young

to   control

their

germs

but

too   old

to   stop

the   hair under

their

skin   and

too   old

to

be   kind   and

sincere   like   you

you're

too   old

to

be   sincere   you   try

despite   your

age   even

if   you   can't

be   true

and

sincere   like

little   ones

when

they   try

to

express what they want or

what they   like

            or   don't

            like

            like

              i

    want   dis

            or

              i

            like

  dat

                          true

        and   sincere

            like

  that

            or like

      when

      they want   something

      they can't

  have   but   really

                                                 really

        want

        can   i   um

        can   i   um

        can   i

  have

  dat   sing   um

        can   i   um

        can   i   um

        can   i   please

  have

  dat   sing   um

        can   i   please

                                                       please

                                                       please

            or   even

when
    they   get
a   little older
          but   still
say   things
      like

a humpback whale is the biggest fish

      or

gasoline is for cars
vaseline is for   people

      or

don't touch me

         true
    and   sincere
      like
that   unlike
    the   surly
                      older

kids who don't seem
     to
know
how   to   say what they mean
          i
      mean
        like you
know   like you
know   what   i
      mean

no   i

don't   i

don't

know   what   you

                        mean

            what   like

        no

        way   i

                    mean   you

know   like you

know

                                    like

        no   you

    don't

know   what they mean

        to   say   at   all

        do   they   even

know

        do   they   even get

                    what they

            say

    or

    do   they

                    have

    no   way

        of

knowing   the   older

                                    you   get

                        the   less simply

                                    you

            say what   you

                        mean

        to . say   you   simply

    don't   say what   you

                        mean

                    any   more

                              even

                    if   you   try

                              and

                    i   try because

          the   more

                         you

     say   the   less

                    you   end

                         up

          meaning   as

               you   get older

                              and

                    even

               if

               i

know   more

                         and   more

                         and

               have   more

                         and   more

     to   say what   you

          say   becomes

                              less simple

                         and   becomes

                              simply

               "like"

               it   becomes

                                   "more

     or   less"

which is
why   i
     stay young or
     try   to

stay young   at least

in   how

i   look

in   the mirror hair long like

hers

ok

so

not   as   long

as   hers

or   as   beautiful

or   as   full

as   hers   but

long

for   me

which isn't   very

long

i   know   but

at least

not   bald

don't

let   me   go   bald

please

stay   dear   hair   but

if

you   go   if

i   have

to   go   bald

please

let   it

be

on

my   face

beardless

beautiful

young   like

                    hers   like
         a   woman
              how
     i
wish   don't
              we   all   that
     i   had
         a   woman's
                                        face
     in   the mirror   like
         you

just put on aftershave always clean
     put
       it in   your
                 palm
                              he said
                                   that's
       it
just   like
                                   that
                         then   slap
       it on   that's
       it
       but   gently
                                          let
                         me
         show   you
              and   he   gently
                              slapped   his face
just   like
                              that
                         he said
just

don't start fussing with your hair
                    your   facial
                    hair
          is   different
                    you   can
          fuss   with your   face
                         that's
                    ok
          just
don't   fuss   with
                    the   hair
on   your   head
                    or   give
                    yourself
        a
          fussy   hair
do   and   become
  one   of   those
          fussy   artist types
               who   grows
               his   hair   and   become
  it   because
               in   the   end
                    you'll   become
  one   of   those
          fussy   faggot   artists
                                        and

there is no room for those
          in   business and
          no
               room for
them   in   my   house
               for   that
                                      matter

                    touchy   men
          who   like
      to   play
          house   don't belong
      in   business   Sam
                          and   i'll
                              have
          you
          know   that   i'll
                              have
          no   touchy   men
      in   my
      room   excuse
                              me
                                  i
                              mean
          no   touchy   men
      in   my   business   because
      in   business
there is   absolutely
          no   excuse
          for

clowning around
              which is funny not because
clowns   are   funny   they
      aren't   but
                      because when
                  i   shave
                              just
              like   every
      man   who   shaves
                          the   white
                              foam
          around   my   red

                        lips   makes
            your   lips   look
                        like
clown   lips   on
            a
clown's   painted   white
                                            face
                              the   mask
                        of   every
            man

humiliated in the morning for
            the   sake
                        of   being
                        taken   seriously
                        later   on
                                    is   that
                                                what
            it   takes   to
                              be
                        taken   seriously
                                    seriously what   does
            it   take   what   do
            i   need
                                                to   do
                                                to
                              be
                        taken   seriously   wear
            this   red and white
                                                        mask
                                                        each
            morning   is   that
            it   wear
            this
humiliating   red and white

                                                            flag
                    of
          a

Canadian maple leaf falling or Japanese
                              sun bleeding
                    or   Swiss coo
                                              coo
                                                    cross
                    or   Polish

sausage i could really
          go   for
  a
sausage   right now
  a   big   breakfast
sausage   instead
          of   the usual shit
      i   eat
          for   breakfast   with
                              the sun   rising
                    as   usual
          for
    you   to
                    eat   shit
                        instead
          of
  a   great big   American
                    breakfast
sausages

pancakes
  a   stack of them with hot syrup beside eggs prepared however you like
and
  a   hot   cup

                    of   coffee

and

a   cup
            of   juice all

served by an
        American waitress who
                waits   on you
                and
serves   you quickly because
        Americans   always get
            what   they
            want
            and   they
                        won't
            wait   long   they
            want .   their meal
        and   they
            want
                it   now   because
            that is   the
        American way
            a   dream
                                                    meal
served by a   hot
            waitress who
                    won't   let
                        you   sit for
                    long
                as   you   dream
            that   she sits
                    on you   for
            a   quicky   while
                    you
            wait   for

your   meal   God
if
only
you
could   dream
the

way
an
American   dreams
you

should move to the States
there's   a
market for
my   work in
the States   i'm sure
there   is   some
market
to   keep
me   busy
there
should   be enough
business
there   for
my   work   and all
work   and
no   pay
here   makes
me   a   dull
kid
when   i'm sure
i   have
enough   solid
music
to   sell

                              in
              the States   or   maybe
                               i
should   sell
   out   and
                                              sell
    my   music
         to the

movies just like novelists turn their
              novels   into screenplays
                        or   poets
                  turn   into
              novelists   to   make
money just   fluff
                                    up
               the
              novel   for
               the
movie   make
               it   realistic
    as   they   say and
    as   realistic
    as   they   want

so people will come and cry
for   a   nice evening
  of   sentimental porn
       with   a   lush   soundtrack
  of   sax
            and   violins

         like   the
movie   they   made   from that
         novel

The Latin Patient is that
                what
                        it was called or
                        was
                        it

In the Skin of a Pussy

                    is that
                        it

In the Skin of a Pussy
                Cat

well no matter
        what

                    the States
should   have
                        a
                        market for
        my   music

unlike this
        socialist dump that doesn't produce
                            results
    like the   States and even
    if   we   could
                                    make
    it   big
                                here
                                and
                                make   some
                                                    money

here

    at   home

the

    Socialists   would

         take

it   all   away leaving

no

                                  c
                                  h
                                  o
                                  i
                                  c
                                  e

     but

      to   leave for

the   States   or

               stay here

               where

               there

    is   nothing

      to

      do

     but   sulk   about

the   dumpy   state   of

this

    quasi

    socialist   country

    and   about

the   bigger

    and   better

grades the US will

      always

   get   because

   the US will

          always
be   an A+ country
          A+   or   D-
                depending
                on   who's
grading   but
          you   need extremes
                         to   make anything
                                          great
                              as

opposed
  to   the same old B+
     we   get year in
                year   out just another
          B+   country   seriously
                              why
     is   everyone
                              here
ok   with
     a   B+
     as   if
          we're   all
ok   with   just
                being
     so
     so   and   why   on
                earth
  do   i   still live
                in   this
                country and   like
                it   even   love
                it

     when

we're not even smart enough

to   be   Marxists

and

not   nearly rich

enough   i   wish

i   had

enough   money

to   be

a   Marxist   but

it

takes

a

lot.   Marx   had

a

lot

of   money

and   when

he   didn't

he'd   mooch

it   because

he   was

smart   that   way

wasn't

he

clever   that

Karl

and   rich

enough

to

sit every day

to   compose

the   Manifesto all

the   time

in

the   world
to   grow his dirty beard
                                            and
                write
                    workers
            of
the   world
            unite
                                    what
if
it   were
            composers
of
the   world
sit   down
                no
            composers
                of
the   world
sit   down   at
the   piano
                                        doesn't
                        sound
                quite   right
                no

we'll   never   be
        clever   enough
        for   Marx's
                                    opium
        of   the   mooches
                                            and
                you
            are
        not

a   mooch.

            you   think
    to   yourself   in
            the   mirror
      even   though
            you   make
    no   money   and
        she   makes
                        it   all
      for   both
      of   you   and
we   can't
                            make

money off
        of
money   for just letting it
                    sit there like Father
                    the   bastard
                                and we'll never
            be   as   great
                                as
                    the   States
        so   we

trash the States and
      the state   of
      the States and
      the   poor
          taste   of
      the States and   how
      the States   keeps
      their   war going
                  to   keep
      the

rich

rich   and

        their   poor

                                 poor

                        and

        the

rich   and

        the   poor

                        and

        the

rich   and

        the   poor

                        and

        the   war

                        and

        the   war

                        and

        the   war

                        and

        the   war

                                 keeps   going

                                        so

                                 we

trash   the States

                        for   being

rich   because

                of

        the   war

    which   keeps   going   because

                of

        the

rich

    which   is   nothing new

                                                    because

                                 as   long

                              as
               we're   not
                              as
rich   as
      the States   we'll   bla
                                                           bla
                                                           bla
                                                           blame
      the States   as   if
      the latest   war
                         were
      the   only   reason
                                                        for
      the States   being
rich   bla
                                              bla
                                              bla

what nonsense
what noise   passes for truth even
               if   there is
                                  some
                    truth
      to   it
      to   pass   it   off
           as   the   whole
                    truth   so   help
                              me
                              is   utter
      nonsense   even
               if   i

don't especially
          like the States but
          like   most

                    others
    i
don't   like the States   mostly because
    i'm
    not   there
    in   the   land
                                        that
                                  hands   you
                              so   much opportunity
                                                    for
    no   reason
            other   than   being
            there   just
                                                for   being
                                  an

American in
America
              everything's free
          in
America   for
      a   small
                    fee
          in
America

    ha
    ha Bernstein
what
    a
    shark   too bad for the
                    words
    that   turned his
                              music
          into

that   shitty

                                                  musical

                              they

                        do

that   words

                        they

                                    turn   pieces

                        of   music

            into   pieces

                        of   shit   but

                        then

                        where

                        others   hear

a   hit   so

            to   speak you

                                                  hear   pure

                                          musical

                  crap   by

      Leonard

      Bernstein   luring people

            in   with   lyrics

one little kid
one little kid
            i   wish he hadn't told
me   really

                                          if   you

had   to

have   words

            in   your

                                    music

                                          if   you   were

                        forced

            to   hear

                    music

          with

words   you'd rather

                        hear

                              the

blues

    woke up this morning

etc   beats

      the   hell out of

      the

                        potato

                        potahto

                        tomato

                        tomahto

                              lyrics

            of   Ira Gershwin poor George

let his brother destroy almost

                    all

  his   music with cutesy pies how

                    much

      better   music

    is   without   any Iras

                              summertime and

          the   lyrics

    is   stupid

                                          and

          the

same goes for opera from Monteverdi

          to   Verdi killing music with sentimental melodrama

          opera

          opera

    God

save   us

            from the plague

       of

    opera

                       with

                    its

   words   unless

they're Howlin Wolf's and just

                do

the   do

      like

  he   says

      words   searching for pleasure

                    in

    how

they   suffer not

                 for

the   leisure

              of   airy

                          fairy

                  supper   music but

              for   truth

           in   music

          since   music

        is   truth

                      truth

                 music

  yes   truth

                     on

the   air

              for

three minutes

    i   want

three minutes   on the radio

      i   don't

          want   my fifteen

    minutes

      i   want

three minutes   times

          fifteen   million people

        by

      their

        radios   listening to

         my   music

        all   at

    once   my   music

    on the radio   times all

      fifteen   million people

          listening

at

  home or

at

  the   corner store

    or

  the   barber secretly

at   work   letting Purple Rain

        into their

        ears

  my   own

    Purple Rain   feeling a

        way

    into

the   corners   of

      their

      ears

  working   secretly on

      their   feelings till

they

let   their   feelings

out   in a

tear

at

the   barber

or   secretly

at

home

my   very   own

Purple Rain

let's   call it

it Purple Pain

my   main   piece

my   big

hit

Purple Pain   owning   a   piece

of

them   with

its

purple   feelings

a

s
e
n
t
i
m
e
n
t
a
l

virus

stored   in

                                        their
                                        ears   till
    the   tears
come   out
                                            and
    my   Purple Pain

may not even
        be
            very good it
may   very   well
        be   pathetic
            with   pathetic lyrics but
                        they   hear
                it   enough times like
        every   U2 song
                        they   hear
                it   drunk
                        enough times
                    at
                    the   bar

        or

                    at
                    the

            store
        or
    the   barber
        or
at
home   that
                                they
                    secretly
come   to
            love   it   and

                                        feel
    my   Purple Pain   fill
them   as
                                        they

hear my
    music that
            Father can't appreciate
        with   his   tin
    ear   has   no
        music   in
                            him
                not   one
                            ounce
    or   28.349 grams
                    of
            the
        music Mother
        must   have
            had
            that
            Father
        with   his
                        tin
    ear   can't
hear   yet
            he
            had
            her   how
                    on
    earth   were
            they   together
        Mother
        with   her
            faith   in

music   and
          Father
     with   nothing
                                                      but
                    his
     faith in
          the   money
          he   prays
               to

religiously
          you know that's
                    the
     only   - thing those communists were
                                        right about
               he   says
religion   is
          the   opium of
          the   asses
                                   says
          the   hypocrite
                                             as
                                              if
               he   weren't
religious   about

praying to his money
               every day afraid
     the money   gods will take
     it   all   back
          one   day   with   interest
                              so
     it   goes with
          money
     it's   all   bull

bull
bull
bull

take
take
take
take

then one day
the big
bad bear
takes
it all back
so
he
prays to
it every day
prays to
the bull
and
the bear
and
to Merrill
and
to Lynch
afraid
it will
all
go
to hell as
he clings
to
it

like a cross insecure
like everyone with

a cross on   his
   or   her   chest
          secure   only
        in   their cleavage
             where   the
   cross   hangs
   for   lucky Jesus
        in   Layla's
              chest
          secure
        on   the
   cross

a noose would have been less popular
                              he
          hanged   for
   our   sins
        who
   could   love
a   hanged   god   with
a   limp
                                   body
                    rather
        than   arms
        and
        hands   stretched
   out   of   love
                    to
        save
   our   sins
        thank   God   she's
              less   into
              God
        than   into

sex i'd never
     have
sex   with
     her
  if   she loved Jesus more than
        me

how can she honestly wear that cross
how can
    an   OB
                         or
  any   MD
                       for
             that
             matter
      honestly wear
  a   cross   even if
                      it's from
   her   mother
  and   of   sentimental
                       value
               from
  her   mother

calling her
    every day
        how's
          work
      Layla
       how   are you feeling
      Layly
       how's   this
               and
       how's   that
               and

                how's   Sam   what's
     he   up   to
   when   if
                you   read   between
     the
   lines   between
     the   pauses
                you're   sure
                              it's really
                         what's
                        that dead
                               beat   doing
                   with
                    his   life
                and
   even   if

she's not all that religious
     isn't
       it   heresy
                    against   medical science
       to   be
               religious
              at
     all   let alone wear
     a   cross

anyone
  who   loves Jesus has wanted
        to
  or   even
                    wants
        to   have   sex   with
           Jesus   and   i'd
                       never

                    have   sex with
anyone
who   wants
anyone
    more   than   me
                        even   if
                                i'm number
        one
        on   the   list in
                            her   mind
                    and
            Jesus   is   second say
                                                    or
                                                    eighth
                            i'd
                    hate
        to   have
        to   share   her   i
                    want
                    a   list
                            with
            just   me   in
                                                    mind
            just   me
                    and   no   other
                    men   or
                    sexy   prophets
        of
        love   and
                    hate   with
                            their   dirty beards
                        even   though

i've seen the way
    she   looks

at

the   hairy ones

as

if   she   wanted

some   unkempt Jew

or   Muslim

is   the   opposite

of   unkempt

kempt   do

they   say   kempt

as

in

he

is   a   kempt

man

or

she

is   kempt

what   does

she   want

a

b
e
a
r
d
e
d

Nazarite

or some   kind

of   religious

hairy

hair   Nazi

i'd   hate

for

her   to
                                      be   religious
i   don't
                              want   to
see
her   veiled
                              in
                    some   sheitel
            or   chador
                                                              oh
                                          no definitely
                                          not
                    a   chador
                    a   chador
is   way   more
                    than
                    a   sheitel
                              and
                    a   sheitel
is   in   no
            way   adorable
                              and
she   knows
i   adore
    her   hair   and
                              want
    her   to
            look
        at   me
          the way
she   looks
        at

Father
    at

the dinner
          table eyes
the silver   smells
 his   rich
after   shave
the   table
          set   for
her   to
          sit   closer
                                to
him   than   you sitting
                        across   from
them   and
          saying   little
          as   little
                            by   little
he   gets
                        closer
                            to
her   with
his   close
              shaven
              face   to
          tell
her   a   little   something
here   a   little   something
there   as
she   laughs
              with
 him
at
the   table   and
              eyes
his
    silver   hair

                    and
                    faces
him   so
she   can   get
                        closer
                    to
him   and   your
                                                    i
                                                    n
                                                    h
                                                    e
                                                    r
                                                    i
                                                    t
                                                    a
                                                    n
                                                    c
                                                    e

unless it all goes
        to   the SPCA
in   his   will
        to   spite you leaving
        it all
        to   cats
        he   never gave
        a
shit   about dogs that
                                          would
                              be   just like
        him
        to   leave
        it all
        to   dogs

but you don't want his money like her
                    i
          mean
    you do   want
          it
    you   just
        don't want
              to   inherit
          it   from
              him   of   course
    you   want   money   just
                        like her
but you   want
              to   make
    your   own
              and   have
    your   own
    you're   just   bad
          at
          it   i
          mean
    you   just
        don't   have
                        the
                  money   making   skills
                        he   has
                        in
              his   blood
though
    you'd   like
              to   inherit
                  them
          and   make
    your   own

yourself

what are

you   doing with

yourself   Sam

.he asks across

the   table

when

he   knows full

well that i

work   on my

music every day

even   if

no   one

will   play it

so   that

he   can

go

on   and pretend

i

don't

work

why

don't

you

play   something for

us

he   says

pointing

to   the grand

he can't play

and   hasn't tuned since

the   day

i   moved out

you used

to   play   all.

    the

time   so much like

    her   at

    the   piano

                    you   wouldn't

remember but she used

        to   play every

                day

                    bastard

        he   knows i can't

remember   how   could

                        i   possibly

    she   would   have loved

                            you

    he   says

    to   Layla beside

                    him

                        you

        used

    to   be   so

talented Sam

        he   says

            seriously what are you doing with yourself

        he   asks

    when

    the   bastard knows

                        your

            hands

            are   too

            sore   to

        play   in   public

anymore you're

a   composer for God's

sake

ok so

you're   not Bach but

who

composes   like

Bach

anymore   when

you   listen

to

Bach's

works

you   see

God   but

yours   leave

you   feeling nothing

but

sore

he's got
the   whole world
why   is
it
"got"
he's
"got"
the   whole world   in
his   hands
why   isn't
it
"holds"
he   "holds"
the   whole world

                who   "has"

    the   world
              or   has

      "got"
    the   world
              or

      "gets"
        it   let alone

                  in
                  his   hands   no to
                            have
                          and   to
          hold   . are
        two   very different things
                        when   your
                        hands   ache unless
    they   hold

    her legs touch
    her   under wait did
    he   just
                            did
    he   just
                              just

          touch
    her   under
    the   table
          touch   his
        leg   against
    hers   and
    she   just
        let   him
                  what   is   this
                          a   romantic dinner for
    them   .   and   what

are

you

the   third   wheel

and   who

the   hell does

he   think

she is

one of his

so   called "friends"

he   used

to   bring

home   for

the   night

                                        Sam say hello

to   my

                friend   Magda

                                or   whatever their names were

isn't he cute

he'd   always

                say

        to

them   leave

me   alone

but   haven't seen

                any   Magdas for years

no   hanky

                                                panky getting

                                        old   i guess

                so

        why

always   with

                        Layla

                every   chance

he   gets

don't say anything
   it's   innocent
                  she'll insist
                        if you
     say anything
or   she'll
     deny
  it   altogether
  as   if you   didn't
               see   them
                        touch
               well   you   didn't exactly
               see
  it   you
               sensed   them
do it   you   didn't   need
                             to
               see
  it   to   know
               all   you   needed was
                             to
               see   them   sitting
                        together
          innocent
                  she'll
     say   innocent
          my   ass
          innocent
     as

the dirty things you know
he   wants to whisper
          in

her   ear like

              what's

        your   favourite position

                                        pause

    at

the   hospital

        sly

    that   pause

              and

              can

        i   see

        your   cross

              and

the

dirty jokes he tells

              at

        the   table always

                    toward

        her   never

              to   me   his

                    eyes

              always   looking for

        the   laugh desperate

                              for

        her   to   laugh with

                    him

              any   reason

                        for

        her   to   look

                    in

              his

              eyes

        he's   desperate

    i   know

i   know

    he's   desperate   and

              old   but

                          it's   no

                        reason

        to   be

     a

dirty   old   prick

have you heard this one already

          chances

  are you

have   so   act surprised like

   you   never

    heard

     it   before

   he   won't   know

    it's

an   old joke

  you   knew

       already

   he's   old

    so   let

   him

have   a   chance to   be   stupid

       and   tell

      it

  where   else

         will

  he

have the   chance

    the   lonely   old

     man

have you heard   it

    go

        ahead   let

               him
have   his   stupid fun

please tell it
           she says God help me
         i   think
                 ok
         he says   sitting up
                      in
                      his   chair
              a
teacher   gives
          her   students
          a   problem
                                    to   solve

"there
  are
three birds on
  a   wire all
three   fly
          away
           why"
                      she asks
then
  a   boy   answers
                      "because
          wires
  are   not safe"
he   says
                          "no"
                          says
the   teacher
"they   fly

                    away   because

        a   boy

like you shoots at them with
                    a   b
                                b
                                gun
                                but
i
like   the   way
    you   think"
        she   says
                                         so
              then
              the   boy gives
              the   teacher
            a   problem
          to   solve
                                              "teacher"
              he   says

"there
  are
three women with
              an   ice cream cone
                              one
              licks
        it   one sucks
        it
    and   one
                  eats
        it   which
                  one   is married"
    he   asks
        and

the   teacher answers

"the   one   who
                                    sucks
        it   of course"

"no"
    says the boy
                "it's
        the   one with
        the   wedding
                        ring
            on   but
            i   like
        the
    way   you think"

not bad
not   very funny but
not bad   the pervert
no   style to
                            it
            but
            then
            he   isn't an artist
                        is
            he   just
                    a   business
                    man
                    and
                    a   pushy
            pervert   with
no   style   and
no   art
        but

his Playboys to

lift   jokes from pathetic telling dinner

        jokes from

his Playboys to

 lift

his   spirits

   a   little and

              the   little

                       spirits

                in

his   little

       old   dick

lifting

  a   pathetic

     joke   i   can

           tell   it's

       from

  Playboy   because

                 i   read

          that   one

            in   one

      of

his Playboys

as a boy

       so   what

 if   i   read

  Playboy   then   i   read

                    it

  a   lot   but

                 i   read

                 it

as a boy   and

      so   what

 if   i   read

  Playboy   now

                              i   read
                              it
        a   little   but
                              i   read
                              it
as   a   boy   he's
                    the
                    pathetic   one
lifting
his   only
            jokes from   there still   better
            to   read
                    that
                    than
                    the

filthy newspaper getting
    the
filthy news   print under
    my   skin every day
                    on
    my   hands
                         i   have to wash
    the   cheap
                    ink
                    i   can't
                             stand
                    on
    my   hands
                                          and
                under
    my   skin   and
                         i   can't
                             stand that
                    i've

got   to
                              have
the newspaper   every day   with
                                                        its
                    daily
filth   so   i
try   to wash
my   hands
            even   if
            i   can't   always
        get
them   clean
                        and   clear
my   mind   of
the   so   called
    "news"

about those teenagers
    who   wanted
    to   behead
        the   prime minister that's not news seriously
    who   hasn't
            wanted
    to   either
            be   or
            behead
        the   prime minister   or
        the   president
            and
        they   call
                        that   news

the shit
they   write
the   opinions

they   have and

the   assholes

they   hire

    to

        write

them   since

                any asshole

                    can

                have an

        opinion   and

                any asshole

                    can

        write

    shit   so

hey   why   not

                    have   asshole

        writers

    shit   asshole

                    opinions

            in   asshole   columns

                    or   blogs online

hey   look

                                        at   me look

                                        at   me

        i   think

        i   can

        write   and

        i   have

            opinions   online

                    and

        i   think

i'm so clever and

    so

    do   W

X
Y
and Z who linked to
me   and
my   clever   posts
                    like
    "re
    read   Ulysses
                    last   night
        and   sight
        read
    all   of   Ligeti's piano études
            now
i   knew
                        was
    clever   but
            who   knew
i'm   even
    cleverer   than
i   thought
            like
        wow"

            what
    shit   any asshole
                    can   blog
                    and
                    any asshole
                    can
            have
                a   column
                            but
the   biggest
                    asshole
        in

the   end   is   you
                                              since   you

  eat it all up
read   every comment
                              and
              every   review in
                                    minutes
      it   takes one
                              minute   to
read   a   review
        a   reviewer   took
          merely   one   hour
      to   write
                                    on   something someone
                                          took
years   to
create   and   you
read
     it all   and
  eat it all up   because
                              in   the
                    end   you
are   the

freshest fish for supper
                    bon appétit
          he   says
                    no   thanks
      i   say
                                  but
                        it's
fresh
          he   says

                    it's
        not   the
fish
   i   say
                    then
                    what
   is   it
   he   **asks**
   i   just mean
        no   thanks
   i   have
        no
            appetite   but
                    thanks
                    anyway
   i   say   although
   i'm   hungry
        you   mean
                to
                    say   that
   i   buy
                    the
freshest fish   in
                    the   market
        he   **says**
                to
        her
                    the   very
best
        he   **says**
                    and
   he   has
        no
            appetite
        he   **says**

to

her   beautiful face

                              it's   delicious

she   says

looking straight
     into   his eyes
                    thank you
          he   says
looking straight
     into   hers
                    and   then
                                 the   perv has
                                 the   nerve   to
                                              ask
          me   if
                                                    i'm
                                                          upset
                    about   something
                    and   then   .   tell
          me   i
look

awfully thin
     well   i
     feel
awful
          how
          do   you
     feel
                    what
a   question
                    what
a   stupid
                                   stupid

                         question
                                         are
           you   seeing
                that   doctor
                                                  anymore
                     he asks
                                         i don't   need
                that   doctor
        i   **say**
well   how
                about   money
                do you   need
                                         more   here take
                                              some
                     he   **says**
                                         i don't   need
        it
        i   **say**
                                                        here
                     he   **says**
                                         i don't   need
                                         any
        i   **say**
                you   need
                                              money
                                         everyone needs
                                              money
                     he   **says**
                                         Sam   baby
                                                   she
                                         says
                                                        take
                the   money
                                                   she
                                         says

                            don't

                be

                                              silly

                                        take

        it

                                        she

                        says   which

                                        makes

        you   want

                        to

                                                    s
                                                    c
                                                    r
                                                    e
                                                    a
                                                    m

                        but

        you   simply

                        say no
                                no

thanks

                        is

            what

        you   say

well   anyhow

it's delicious

        she says to him

as   his hand nears

                            hers

        they   don't quite touch
                            but

        they   would love
            to   wouldn't
        they   love

to   touch

      each

other at

the   table

just

as   you

would love

to   punch

him   in

the   mouth

or

for

him   just   once

to

be   kind

to   you

too   but

no

no

no   just   stupid questions

for   you

like

how

do   you feel

what

a

joke he must think you're

just   another

one   of

his

thin   pathetic dinner

jokes   sitting

at

                    the   table
            when
    he   turns
                                to
            her   beautiful face
                                to
                    ask   if
    she's

heard
the   one about
the   goat
            that sucks
the   stick
he   winks
                i
        have
    to go
        you   say and
        you   better
    before
he   makes
        you   sick
the   old   lech
                            even if
        you hate
    to   leave
                    them
    alone   together
        go
ahead   let
                her
            suck
            up
    to   him   when

you   leave

                                           if

she   wants

     to   suck

                  up

     to   him

     for   his

money   fine

                        let

                   her   but

        you have

     to   get

              up   from

the   table

                        and   finally

                              leave

        what

        about

dessert don't you want

              any

              he says

              when

        you're   almost

        out   the

door   the   silver butter knife

        you   just   filched

        up

        your   sleeve

           what   are

        you   doing Sam

              where   are

        you   going

              she says

        and

          you   hate

     to   leave

                    her

                    here   but

   don't you want

some babka i bought

               you

          a

     babka

                    the

          pig   he knows

               i

love babka   but

          has   the   nerve

                         to   mention

               it   only

                                        once

               i'm   leaving

so   they   can

                                                    eat

                         the

     babka   just

                    the   two

of   them   with

                    her   all

                         to   himself

                         but   Sam baby

               you

love babka

                    she   says

                         it's   true

          i bought   it

                         for

               you

he   says
when
he knows

i need to
    get back home and
    get   down
                one
                more
    bar   or   maybe
        a   few
        more   down
            on   paper
                                after
i   put
            down   the

knife what
        are you going to pawn
    it   or   cut
        your   wrists seriously
    why   did
        you   take
    it   you
        should   put
            down   .   the blade Sam

you've gone
        over
your   face again
            and
            again
            and
            perfection is the .
                    no   what's

the   line obsession

that's

it

obsession

is the   hobgoblin

of   fools

and

you   should

wash your hands again did

you

wash your hands   before

you   started shaving

i hope

i   started   clean

t
h
i
s

m
o
r
n
i
n
g

maybe

i'll   manage

a   few   bars

maybe

more   once

i'm   clean

and   shaven

and   seated

                                                            at
        the   piano
                again

a baby again
at   the piano with everything black
                    and white
a baby   faced
  baby   feeling weak
as
a baby again   when   you can't
                                    face   feeling
                everything
                    hinge
            on   everything   else
                with   nothing
                            black
                and white   in
        the   world
                                                    except
        the piano
                and   skunks
                it's
                                                                    t
                                                                    r
                                                                    u
                                                                    e
                                                        skunks
                        are   also
                    black
        and white   but
                                        nothing
                                        else
            and   there's   nothing
                                    you can

do about
     it
so   why don't
   you   cry
   about
     it
go   ahead
    put
   your   head
        on
      the   piano
       and cry
   about   what
   you   can
do   nothing
   about
go   ahead   cry
   your   Purple Pain
      at
    the   piano
    and   compose
   your   own   sentimental
        music
go   on
   and cry
   when
 you   feel
 you   can
do   nothing   like

that time when
   i   could think of
     nothing but
   the   war period
    nothing   else

but war

war

war

war

war

war

war

war

war

war

war

war

war

war

war

war

war

war

war

war

war

war

war

war

war

war

war

war

war

war

war

war

war

war

war

war

war

war

war

war

war

war

war

war

war

war

war

war

war

war

war

war

war

war

war

war

war

war

war

war

war

war

and

then
the   war   came to
  an
  end   well
that   part
            of
the   war   came to
  end   for
            now
  and
i   could think of   something
                            else   like

fast cars and women
  is   that really
                  what's
        on
          my
          mind   when i shave now
  is   that really
                  what's
        on
          men's
          minds   when
          we   shave   there's
                              no   way
            that   all
            that's
        on
          my
          mind
  are women   with
                              their
                              hair   blowing
                                          in

fast cars   with

          open   roofs

                                                          in

                                    the
          open   air

as   i   drive
fast   and   they   drive
          me   wild
                                    with
                                    their
                                    hair   blowing
                                                          into

          mine

as   they
          open   their

     arms
          and   spread   their
                                         no there
is   no   way
                    that   i have
                    that

     on
          my
          mind

although he must
          the   dirty old man you know
          he   wants
          her   and
          she   wants
          his   dirty   money   maybe
                              your
                    money
                              one   day

     though

all   his   for

                              now

                    and

who   knows   if

                    you   want it   even

                                if

                                              s
                                              e
                                              c
                                              r
                                              e
                                              t
                                              l
                                              y

                    you

          do   no

all   you know   for   sure

     is   that

there

  are millions of people wanting

          to be   loved

     millions of people waiting

          to be   held many

          of   them   women

                                    many

          of   them   pictured naked

                    waiting   for you

          to   love   and

                    wanting   you

          to   hold

                    them

sad really when you

          think

                    about
          .   it   ·that

there
they
  are   pictured   like
                                           you
                         now   nearly
                                      naked
                in
the   mirror   ·
               wanting
          to   be   . held

by their mothers .
    the   lucky Jesuses or
                       is
                       it
                  Jesi   born in
      their mothers'   arms and all
      the   lucky   Oedipusses
                            or .
                     is
                     it   Oedipussies (
                         lying
                         in
      their mothers'   laps
         no   fat
                                                 fathers
      there   .   to
               fuck   .   with
      their   lives
                                       just
      their mothers   alive
                         and

                              well
                         and
          there   to   hold
      their

hand sore again from writing just
          one   bar
and   stuck
          on   the
                                    twelfth
                    just   hanging
          over   the
                                    twelfth
                    bar
                    as   if
                                    the   whole piece will
                    be
          over   in   twelve
                    bars   like
          some   tame
                                                         little children's

          song
          or

that pinball machine jingle on Sesame
                         Street
                              1 2 3 4 5 6 7 8 9
                              10
                              11
                              12
that   infernal
                    jingle

you'll never get
    out   of

your   head and
you'll
      never get
  out   of
your   hands
  all   that
you   have   in
                    mind
                    and
you'll never get   into
your   head
  all   that   matters
                    in
              the   world
                        so   maybe
  one   last short piece
                                  is
  all
you   have   left
              in
you   and   maybe
              that   last   piece
                                  is
  all   that
will   last
        of
you   in
              the   world
              in
              the
              end   but
              that's
              a   big
                        maybe
                  so

never   mind

    posing as
              some important
composer
composing   important
compositions   when
              a   magnum opus
         is   obviously hopeless
         some   magical
                        hocus
                        pocus   ·   useless
                        to   hope   for
              when

twelve bars may be
              enough if
              you   repeat
                        them
              enough   times
                        like
                        Steve Reich
              or
    a
twelve bar   blues
                        really
twelve bars may be
              enough   and
                        at
                        least
twelve   fans
    even   if
              you'd   rather   fifteen
                                        million
                                        and   hardly

a

        the   lyric since

                                                            lyrics

    repeat   anyway

woke up this morning

            repeat

woke up this morning

                etc

                etc that's easy enough but

                    what

                to   call

                    it   something

                                            catchy

                    it   has

                to   be   something

                                            catchy   if

                    it's   going

                to   be   a

                    hit   you   know

                                            something

                                                    big   like

You Are So Beautiful To Me

                    what an

                        insult

                        just   '

            to me

                            and it's already

    taken   anyhow

            why   not

                    just   leave

                            it

                            at

You Are So Beautiful

            pitiful   then maybe

Beauty

        too

dated   then   call

                  it

You

        too   general

                    then

          Me

        too   personal

                    then

I

  too short practically nothing it's

               so

   short   then   maybe

They

    too distant then something totally different like

Kill The Pig

       come

       on

         now seriously what

      do   you want sausage

I Could Really Go For A Sausage

                  too true

                  too   autobiographical then

      call   it

Untitled

      too modern then

Ununtitled

      too contemporary then

Passacaglia

                        would be

                                    perfect but

                who   calls anything

    a

passacaglia   anymore then what

                about

I Know What You're After

                                    too honest

                            too   paranoid am i

                                    paranoid   i'm not

                                    paranoid   but

                                        am i

                        honest   i'm not   sure maybe

mention California everyone loves

            California   so

                                        try to work

        in California   somehow maybe

mention   the

            California   sun   or

            call   it

The Daylight Sonata

                        too derivative then

Don't Believe The Hype

                very   funny

    but   you

do   believe

        it

don't   you have

        to

        believe   your   own anyway

      to   some degree

          then   make

  it

To The Memory

  Of Her   Spirit

                too precious by far

                too   sentimental keep

                it   simple

In G

    unless i make

        it a   twelve tone piece say

        a   twelve tone

        twelve   bar blues but who will

                  play

        a   twelve tone

        twelve   bar blues   really

                     who   other than you

                    will

             play   what

                              you write

musicians would rather

        do their

          hair

  in   the mirror

than   play

    what

      you   write

        they   all just

want   their   picture

  in   the   paper

      anyway   screw

    the

music   screw

                    the   composer

                                    all

                    they

want   is   fame

        you   think

                                            to

            yourself   fame
and
fancy   hair   pictured
    in   the   paper
                what

    a   bunch

                                                            of

                                                                n

                                                                a

                                                                r

                                                                c

                                                                i

                                                                s

                                                                s

                                                                i

                                                                s

                                                                t

                                                                s

        you   think

                                        to

            yourself

        in   the   mirror   all

self absorbed
        or   is it
self
self   what's
            it   called

self   reflective like an
   ars   poetica hey

Ars Poetica
            that's not
         half   bad for
      a   title but
         it's   too literary then maybe

Farce Poetica
            now that's
               catchy and
                  it's   clever but
                        even   worse
            than   being too literary
               it's   literary
                                             lite   so
         how   about

Parts To Whole
      too   tidy then just plain

Farts
   hey why not spread
   the   joy
                  a   little
            spread   your cheeks
            to   bring
                  a   little
                  joy
            to   your   nose
                        or
                  a   little   smile
            to   your   face and maybe
            to   others

but then you won't
    be   taken seriously will
       you
       you'll
    be   taken   for
           a   clown which
                 of   course
      you   are   who
        isn't
but   to   sell
      your   music
       it   needs
             to
    be   taken seriously
             and   for
       it   to
    be   taken seriously
      you   need
             to
    be   taken seriously
             and   to
    be   taken seriously
      you   need
           a   style
             of
      your   own
             of   course
           and   being
           a   clown
         is
         not
           a   style
      you   own
      you don't
        have

a

patent

on

it

do

you   and   what

would   she

say   about

Farts

Farts

she'd say

that's

what you've been working

on   all this time

Farts

she'd say   over

and   over

that's

what you

have

to

show   for

your   work

that's

what you've   come up

with

Farts

she'd say

Sam   baby

why   didn't

you   call it   Layla

really   who

am i   kidding

it's   time

to

cut

  the crap just don't

cut   yourself

       and   bleed

           to   death

but   it never happens

                              she says

                                 stroking

           your   hands

                          as

                if

                it never happened   come

       on   who

                           am   i   kidding

i don't want

      any titles for my

              music

             music shouldn't

   mean   anything

        still

one   solid   golden

      title   could

   mean

    a   lot

                   to

    a   lot

       of   people

                     people

   want

    a   word

            at   least

      or

    a   few

                              to

                        hang

                    on   to   as

                                      the

              music   changes

                    so   maybe call it

Meander

          sounds too much like

Me

     And

       Her

                        when for all your love

     and   love

         is   the   only   word

                              for

               it   you   know

                              you

     can   only   compose

                              your   self

                              only   what

          is   in

     and   out   of   you

          so   then   maybe

Me

     And

Me

          makes more sense at this point

                              in

                    the   mirror

                but

               is   that too

               self   incumbent

                    what's

                        the
        word   indulgent
            self   indulgent
                                    that's
                it   what's
                        the

matter with you that
                you   can't remember
    a   simple expression
                you   need
    a   cup   of
        tea   to   wake
                up   too   slow right
                                                now
        hey   -   maybe
                    call
        it

Slow
        too *andante*
        too   *adagio*
        too   *lento*
        too   alright quit thinking

about
        titles just choose something
                        so
    you   can
                    get   on with writing
        it   and
                    get   on with
                        the   day
            just   settle
                        on

                    something   short
                              and   simple like

Ow
      really
Ow
            is that
               the best you can do
Ow
            as   in
Ow   that   hurts
            i'm   in   pain help please
                    no   one wants
            a   painful   title
                    and
                    no

                                        one wants
                                        more
                        pain   let alone   another's
                                                              so
              stop   it
                    no   more   titles
                    no   more
                                          words   enough
                        pain

just forget
        it
    for   now
    or   once and
    for   all
      let
        it   go   but where
          to   and

with
    this last
            thought
                    still
with
    him   Sam puts down
    his   blade washes and dries
    his   hands
                                                       and
    his   face turns
                                away   from
        the   sink
                                            and   turns   off
        the

yellow light above the mirror
            before   walking back into
                    the room
                                    past
            the   piano
                            to   stand
                            for a   moment
                        in
            the   sun coming
                        in   now   through
            the   window
        slightly   warming

his body that's barely clothed but
            clothed   enough for any neighbours
                            or   passers
                        by   who   might
                        be   there
                                to   see
his   hands   are

146

fine now at least you can't sense they're sore unlike
earlier
first   thing
in
the   morning but
no   longer
since

he's put down the blade for
the   day
he   must
be   ready
to   write some
more
of
the   music
he's   been working on even
if
he   needs
to   pee   and
eat

breakfast
first with
the usual
mug   of
tea   unless
he   decides for
once
to   have coffee like Layla
always
has

with
breakfast
which   will

it   be   coffee

                    or

tea   which   will

        he   choose there's

                              always

                              a   choice   isn't

                                              there

To the reader

to
the
reader
    in
    thinking all
    things   become solitary and slow
             so   wrote Heidegger
               but
this   is   not
       a   Heideggerian book
          it
          is   non   Heideggaryan   for those
               who   have
read   Heidegger
          and
       i   haven't
read   Heidegger   being
       anti   Heideggerian   after
all   so   as   you
                hold
       it
       let
       it
     become   your
           own
       and
       as   you
read   it
       let
       it
     become
      a
thing   that
thinks   and   if
         not   that

then   at

least   let
                                 it
              be
                   some
         thing
         in   you
                                        that
                   is   always
changing